S[WEET]

DREAMS

When making special garments and accessories for babies, Caron® Simply Soft® yarn is the crocheter's favorite. That's because this ultimately soft, washable yarn is so comfortable and durable. The cozy cardigans, hats, booties, and blankets in this collection of patterns were designed especially for use with Simply Soft, so you know you're creating the very best for Baby.

Leisure Arts, Inc.
Little Rock, Arkansas

big granny baby blanket

 EASY

designed by Reneé Barnes

FINISHED MEASUREMENTS
Width   43"/109cm
Length   43"/109cm

MATERIALS
Caron International's Simply Soft **MEDIUM 4**
(100% acrylic; 6 oz/170g, 315 yds/288m):
#9719 Soft Pink, 5 oz (A)
#9701 White, 4 oz (B)
#9717 Orchid, 6 oz (C)
#9756 Lavender Blue, 6 oz (D)
#9722 Plum Wine, 5 oz (E)

Crochet hook, size US H/8 (5mm), or size to obtain gauge
Yarn needle

GAUGE
In pattern, 7 shells and 14 rows = 8"/20.25cm.

Instructions continued on page 4.

ABBREVIATIONS

beg	beginning
rep	repeat
RS	right side
rnd(s)	round(s)
sk	skip
sp(s)	space(s)
st(s)	stitch(es)

SPECIAL TERMS

beg corner-shell: (2 dc, ch 2, 3 dc) in indicated space.
corner-shell: (3 dc, ch 2, 3 dc) in indicated space.
shell: (2 dc, ch 2, 2 dc) in indicated stitch or space.
tr2tog: Treble crochet 2 together—*[Yarn over] twice, insert hook in next stitch, yarn over and pull up a loop, (2 loops on hook), [yarn over and draw through 2 loops on hook] twice; rep from * once more, yarn over and draw through all 3 loops on hook.

STITCHES USED

Chain (ch)
Double crochet (dc)
Single crochet (sc)
Slip stitch (sl st)

BLANKET

With A, ch 4; join with sl st in first ch to form a ring.

Rnd 1 (RS): Ch 3 (counts as first dc here and throughout), work 15 more dc in ring; join with sl st in first dc—16 dc.

Rnd 2: [Ch 4, tr2tog, ch 4, sl st in next 2 dc] 4 times—4 tr2tog, 8 sl st, and 8 ch-4 sps. Fasten off.

Rnd 3: With RS facing, join B with sc in any tr2tog, ch 4, (tr, ch 4, tr) in sp between next 2 sl st (corner made), ch 4, *sc in next tr2tog, ch 4, (tr, ch 4, tr) in sp between next 2 sl st, ch 4; rep from * around; join with sl st in first sc. Fasten off.

Rnd 4: With RS facing, join C with sl st in any corner ch-4 sp, ch 3, (2 dc, ch 2, 3 dc) in same ch-4 sp (beg corner-shell made), ch 1, (2 dc, ch 2, 2 dc) in next sc (shell made), ch 1, *(3 dc, ch 2, 3 dc) in next corner ch-4 sp (corner-shell made), ch 1, shell in next sc, ch 1; rep from * 2 more times; join with sl st in first dc. Fasten off.

Rnd 5: With RS facing, join D with sl st in any corner ch-2 sp, ch 3, beg corner-shell in same ch-2 sp, shell in next ch-1 sp, ch 1, sk next shell, shell in next ch-1 sp, *corner-shell in next corner ch-2 sp, shell in next ch-1 sp, ch 1, sk next shell, shell in next ch-1 sp; rep from * 2 more times; join with sl st in first dc. Fasten off.

Rnd 6: With RS facing, join A with sl st in any corner ch-2 sp, ch 3, beg corner-shell in same ch-2 sp, *dc in sp between corner-shell and next shell, shell in ch-2 sp of each shell to next corner-shell, dc in sp between last shell and next corner-shell, corner-shell in corner ch-2 sp; rep from * 2 more times, dc in sp between corner-shell and next shell, shell in ch-2 sp of each shell to beg corner-shell, dc in sp between last shell and beg corner-shell; join with sl st in first dc. Fasten off.

Rnd 7: With RS facing, join E with sl st in any corner ch-2 sp, ch 3, beg corner-shell in same ch-2 sp, sk next 3 dc (of corner shell), *shell in next dc, shell in ch-2 sp of each shell to last dc before corner-shell, shell in next dc, corner-shell in corner ch-2 sp, sk next 3 dc (of corner shell); rep from * 2 more times, shell in next dc, shell in ch-2 sp of each shell to last dc before beg corner-shell, shell in next dc; join with sl st in first dc. Fasten off.

Rnds 8–37: Rep Rnds 6 and 7, changing color as in following color sequence: work next rnd with C, 1 rnd with D, *1 rnd with A, 1 rnd with E, 1 rnd with C, 1 rnd with D, 1 rnd with B, 1 rnd with A, 1 rnd with E, 1 rnd with C, 1 rnd with D; rep from * 2 more times, work last rnd with B.

FINISHING

Using yarn needle, weave in all ends.

granny for baby

 **INTERMEDIATE**

designed by Martha Brooks Stein

FINISHED MEASUREMENTS
Width   35"/89cm, including border
Length   44"/112cm, including border

MATERIALS

MEDIUM 4

Caron International's Simply Soft
(medium/worsted weight yarn)
(100% acrylic; 6 oz/170g, 315 yds/288m):
#9712 Soft Blue, 6 oz (A)
#9717 Orchid, 6 oz (B)
#9719 Soft Pink, 6 oz (C)
#9726 Soft Yellow, 7 oz (D)
#9737 Light Country Peach, 6 oz (E)
#9739 Soft Green, 6 oz (F)

Crochet hook, size US I/9 (5.5mm), or size to obtain gauge
Yarn needle

GAUGE
2¹/₄" x 2¹/₄"/5.75 x 5.75cm

ABBREVIATIONS

rep	repeat
RS	right side
rnd(s)	round(s)
sk	skip
sp(s)	space(s)

Instructions continued on page 8.

SPECIAL TERMS

rev sc: reverse single crochet—working from left to right, insert hook in next ch-1 sp, yarn over and draw up a loop (2 loops on hook), yarn over and draw through 2 loops on hook.

STITCHES USED

Chain (ch)
Double crochet (dc)
Half double crochet (hdc)
Reverse single crochet (rev sc)
Single crochet (sc)
Slip stitch (sl st)

NOTES

1. Squares are "joined as you go" while working the second rnd.
2. Joining squares in the order of assembly shown in the assembly diagram ensures that each square will be joined to other squares along at most two sides.

FIRST SQUARE

With A, ch 3; join with sl st in first ch to form a ring.

Rnd 1 (RS): Ch 2 (counts as first dc here and throughout), 2 dc in ring, [ch 2, 3 dc in ring] 3 times; join with hdc to first dc (joining hdc serves as a ch-2 sp)—12 dc (consisting of four 3-dc groups) and 4 ch-2 sps.

Rnd 2: Ch 2, 2 dc in first ch-2 sp (formed by joining hdc), [ch 1, (3 dc, ch 2, 3 dc) in next ch-2 sp] 3 times, ch 1, 3 dc in first ch-2 sp again, ch 2; join with sl st in first dc—24 dc, 4 ch-2 sps, and 4 ch-1 sps. Fasten off.

NEXT SQUARE (make 284 – 47 with A, 44 with B, 45 with C, 50 with D, 48 with E, 50 with F)

Note: Make and join squares in the order indicated on the assembly diagram. The first square is in the upper right corner. Next make and join 2 squares with F, then 3 squares with D, 4 squares with E, 5 squares with C, and so on.

Ch 3; join with sl st in first ch to form a ring.

Rnd 1: Work Rnd 1 of First Square.

Refer to assembly diagram to determine the number of sides of current square that need to be joined to neighboring squares (at most 2 sides), then work the corresponding joining rnd.

Join Across One Side Only: Ch 2, 2 dc in first ch-2 sp (formed by joining hdc), ch 1; 3 dc in next ch-2 sp, ch 1, hold wrong sides of current square and neighboring square together, sc in corresponding ch-2 sp of neighboring square, 3 dc in same ch-2 sp of current square, sc in next ch-1 sp of neighboring square, 3 dc in next ch-2 sp of current square, sc in next ch-2 sp of neighboring square, ch 1, 3 dc in same ch-2 sp of current square (side join complete); work remainder around current square only as follows, ch 1, (3 dc, ch 2, 3 dc) in next ch-2 sp, ch 1, 3 dc in first ch-2 sp again, ch 2; join with sl st in first dc. Fasten off.

Instructions continued on page 10.

granny for baby assembly diagram

106	92	79	67	56	46	37	29	22	16	11	7	4	2	1
121	107	93	80	68	57	47	38	30	23	17	12	8	5	3
136	122	108	94	81	69	58	48	39	31	24	18	13	9	6
	137	123	109	95	82	70	59	49	40	32	25	19	14	10
		138	124	110	96	83	71	60	50	41	33	26	20	15
			139	125	111	97	84	72	61	51	42	34	27	21
				140	126	112	98	85	73	62	52	43	35	28
					141	127	113	99	86	74	63	53	44	36
						142	128	114	100	87	75	64	54	45
							143	129	115	101	88	76	65	55
									130	116	102	89	77	66
										131	117	103	90	78
											132	118	104	91
												133	119	105
													134	120
														135

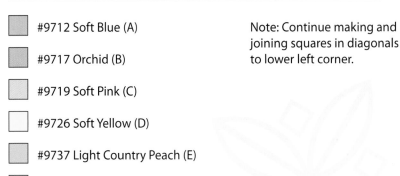

#9712 Soft Blue (A)

#9717 Orchid (B)

#9719 Soft Pink (C)

#9726 Soft Yellow (D)

#9737 Light Country Peach (E)

#9739 Soft Green (F)

Note: Continue making and joining squares in diagonals to lower left corner.

9

Join Across Two Sides: Ch 2, 2 dc in first ch-2 sp (formed by joining hdc), ch 1; 3 dc in next ch-2 sp, ch 1, hold wrong sides of current square and first neighboring square together, sc in corresponding ch-2 sp of neighboring square, 3 dc in same ch-2 sp of current square, sc in next ch-1 sp of neighboring square, 3 dc in next ch-2 sp of current square, sc in next ch-2 sp of neighboring square, ch 1 (first side join complete); hold wrong sides of current square and second neighboring square together, sc in corresponding ch-2 sp of neighboring square, 3 dc in same ch-2 sp of current square, sc in next ch-1 sp of neighboring square, 3 dc in next ch-2 sp of current square, sc in next ch-2 sp of neighboring square, ch 1, 3 dc in same ch-2 sp of current square (second side join complete); work remainder around current square only as follows, ch 1, 3 dc in first ch-2 sp again, ch 2; join with sl st in first dc. Fasten off.

BORDER

Rnd 1: Join D with sc in any corner ch-2 sp of blanket, *ch 1, sk next dc, sc in next dc (middle dc of 3-dc group), ch 1, sc in next ch-sp, ch 1, sk next dc, sc in next dc, ch 1, **sc in corner ch-sp of current square, ch 1, sc in corner ch-sp of next square, ch 1, sk next dc, sc in next dc (center dc of 3-dc group), ch 1, sc in next ch-sp, ch 1, sk next dc, sc in next dc, ch 1; rep from ** across to next corner of blanket ***, (sc, ch 2, sc) in corner ch-sp of blanket; rep from * around ending last rep at ***, sc again in first corner ch-sp of blanket; join with hdc in first sc (joining hdc serves as a ch-2 sp).

Rnd 2: Ch 1, sc in first ch-2 sp (formed by joining hdc), ch 1, [sc in next ch-1 sp, ch 1] across to next corner of blanket, *(sc, ch 2, sc) in corner ch-sp of blanket, ch 1, [sc in next ch-1 sp, ch 1] across to next corner of blanket; rep from * around blanket, sc again in first corner ch-sp of blanket; join with hdc in first sc (joining hdc serves as a ch-2 sp).

Rnd 3: Ch 1, rev sc in first ch-2 sp (formed by joining hdc), ch 2, [rev sc in next ch-1 sp, ch 2] across to next corner of blanket, *(rev sc, ch 2, rev sc) in corner ch-sp of blanket, ch 2, [rev sc in next ch-1 sp, ch 2] across to next corner of blanket; rep from * around, rev sc again in first corner ch-sp of blanket, ch 2; join with sl st in first rev sc. Fasten off.

FINISHING

Using yarn needle, weave in all ends.

striped hoodie

Shown on page 13.
designed by Lisa Gentry

 EASY

SIZES: 3-6 (9-12, 18-24) months

FINISHED MEASUREMENTS
Chest 20 (22, 24)"/51 (56, 61)cm
Length 11 (12, 13)"/28 (30.5, 33)cm

MATERIALS
Caron International's Simply Soft MEDIUM **4**
(100% acrylic; 6 oz/170g, 315 yds/288m):
#9709 Light Country Blue, 6 (6, 12) oz (A)
#9705 Sage, 6 (6, 6) oz (B)

Crochet hook, size US H/8 (5mm), or size to obtain gauge
Stitch markers
Yarn needle
2 buttons—⁷/₈" (22mm) diameter
Sewing needle and matching thread

GAUGE
In Stripe pattern, 8 V-sts (16 dc) and 12 rows = 4"/10cm

ABBREVIATIONS
rep	repeat
RS	right side
sp(s)	space(s)
st(s)	stitch(es)
WS	wrong side

SPECIAL TERMS
V-st (V-stitch): 2 dc in indicated space.

Instructions continued on page 12.

STITCHES USED
Chain (ch)
Double crochet (dc)
Single crochet (sc)
Slip stitch (sl st)

V-st Pattern (multiple of 2 sts + 1)
Row 1 (WS): Ch 1, sc in first st, *ch 1, sk next st, sc in next st; rep from * across, turn.

Row 2 (RS): Ch 3 (counts as dc here and throughout), 2 dc in each ch-1 sp across (V-st made), dc in last sc, turn.

Row 3: Ch 1, sc in sp between first dc and next V-st, ch 1, *sc in sp between next 2 V-sts, ch 1; rep from * across, sc in sp between last V-st and turning ch, turn.

Rep Rows 2 and 3 for V-st pattern.

NOTES
1. To change color, work last st of old color to last yarn over. Yarn over with new color and draw through all loops on hook to complete stitch. Continue working with new color. Carry color not in use up side of piece. Take care to hide the strands of unused yarn when assembling and finishing hoodie.
2. Following bottom band, color is changed every other row to work 2 rows with B, and 2 rows with A throughout.

BACK
With A, ch 40 (44, 48).

Bottom band
Row 1 (RS): Sc in 2nd ch from hook and in each remaining ch across, turn—39 (43, 47) sc.

Rows 2 and 3: Ch 1, sc in each st across, change to B in last sc on last row, turn.

Row 4: With B, work Row 1 of V-st pattern—20 (22, 24) sc, and 19 (21, 23) ch-1 sps.

Row 5: With B, work Row 2 of V-st pattern, change to A in last st—40 (44, 48) dc.

Rows 6 and 7: With A, work next 2 rows of V-st pattern (Row 3, then Row 2 of pattern), change to B in last st on last row.

Rows 8 and 9: With B, work next 2 rows of V-st pattern, change to A in last st on last row.

Rep Rows 6–9 until piece measures 11 (12, 13)"/28 (30.5, 33)cm from beginning. Fasten off.

LEFT FRONT
With A, ch 24 (26, 28).

Work same as for back until piece measures 6$\frac{1}{2}$ (7, 7$\frac{1}{2}$)"/ 16.5 (18, 19)cm from beginning, end with a RS row (Row 2 of V-st pattern). You should have 23 (25, 27) sc when working button band, 24 (26, 28) dc when working V-st rows, and 12 (13, 14) sc and 11 (12, 13) ch-1 sps when working sc/ch-1 sp rows.

Instructions continued on page 14.

Note: Continue to change color every other row throughout.

Next Row (buttonhole): Ch 1, sc in sp between first sc and next V-st, ch 1, sc in sp between next 2 V-sts, ch 3 (for buttonhole), sc in sp between next 2 V-sts, ch 1, *sc in sp between next 2 V-sts, ch 1; rep from * across, sc in sp between last V-st and turning ch, turn.

Next 2 Rows: Work Rows 2 and 3 of V-st pattern, take care to work only one V-st in the ch-3 buttonhole sps.

Rep last 2 rows until piece measures 8¹⁄₂ (9, 9¹⁄₂)"/21.5 (23, 24)cm from beginning; end with a RS row (Row 2 of V-st pattern).

Next Row (buttonhole): Rep buttonhole row.

Next 2 Rows: Work Rows 2 and 3 of V-st pattern, take care to work only one V-st in the ch-3 buttonhole sps.

Rep last 2 rows until piece measures 9¹⁄₂ (10, 10¹⁄₂)"/24 (25.5, 26.5)cm from beginning; end with a RS row (Row 2 of V-st pattern). Fasten off.

Shape Neck

Row 1 (WS): Join yarn with sc in sp between 2nd and 3rd V-st, place marker for hood placement, ch 1, *sc in sp between next 2 V-sts, ch 1; rep from * across, sc in sp between last V-st and turning ch, turn— 10 (11, 12) sc, and 9 (10, 11) ch-1 sps.

Row 2: Ch 3, V-st in next 7 (8, 9) ch-1 sps, dc in next ch-1 sp, leave remaining sts unworked, turn— 16 (18, 20) dc.

Row 3: Sl st in first 3 sts (over first V-st), ch 1, sc in sp between first and 2nd V-st, ch 1, *sc in sp between next 2 V-sts, ch 1; rep from * across, sc in sp between last V-st and turning ch, turn—7 (8, 9) sc, and 6 (7, 8) ch-1 sps.

Row 4: Ch 3, V-st in next 4 (5, 6) ch-1 sps, dc in next ch-1 sp, leave remaining sts unworked, turn—10 (12, 14) dc.

Beginning with Row 3 of pattern, work even in V-st pattern until piece measures same as back. Fasten off.

RIGHT FRONT
With A, ch 24 (26, 28).

Work same as for back until piece measures 9¹⁄₂ (10, 10¹⁄₂)"/24 (25.5, 26.5)cm from beginning; end with a RS row (Row 2 of V-st pattern).

Shape Neck
Note: Continue to change color every other row throughout.

Row 1 (WS): Ch 1, sc in sp between first sc and next V-st, [ch 1, sc in sp between next 2 V-sts] 9 (10, 11) times, leave remaining sts unworked, place marker for hood placement, turn—10 (11, 12) sc, and 9 (10, 11) ch-1 sps.

Row 2: Sl st in first 4 sts (into 2nd ch-1 sp), ch 3, V-st in each remaining ch-1 sp across, dc in last sc, turn—16 (18, 20) dc.

Row 3: Ch 1, sc in sp between first sc and next V-st, [ch 1, sc in sp between next 2 V-sts] 6 (7, 8) times, leave remaining sts unworked, turn—7 (8, 9) sc, and 6 (7, 8) ch-1 sps.

Row 4: Rep Row 2—10 (12, 14) dc.

Beginning with Row 3 of pattern, work even in V-st pattern until piece measures same as back. Fasten off.

SLEEVE (make 2)
With A, ch 22 (24, 26).

Rows 1–7: Work Rows 1–7 of back—22 (24, 26) dc.

Note: Continue to change color every other row throughout.

Row 8: Ch 1, sc in first dc, sc in sp between first dc and next V-st, ch 1, *sc in sp between next 2 V-sts, ch 1; rep from * across, sc in sp between last V-st and turning ch, sc in top of turning ch, turn—13 (14, 15) sc, and 10 (11, 12) ch-1 sps.

Row 9: Ch 3, dc in next sc, V-st in each ch-1 sp across, dc in last 2 sc, turn—24 (26, 28) dc.

Row 10: Ch 1, sc in sp between first 2 dc, ch 1, sc in sp between 2nd dc and first V-st, ch 1, *sc in sp between next 2 V-sts, ch 1; rep from * across, sc in sp between last V-st and next

dc, ch 1, sc in sp between last dc and turning ch, turn—13 (14, 15) sc, and 12 (13, 14) ch-1 sps.

Row 11: Ch 3, V-st in each ch-1 sp across, dc in last sc, turn—26 (28, 30) dc.

Rep Rows 8–11 twice more—34 (36, 38) dc.

Beginning with Row 3 of pattern, work even in V-st pattern until piece measures 7 (8, 9$\frac{1}{2}$)"/18 (20.5, 24)cm from beginning. Fasten off.

HOOD
With A, ch 54 (58, 62).

Row 1: Sc in 2nd ch from hook and in each remaining ch across, change to B in last st, turn—53 (57, 61) sc.

Row 2: With B, work Row 1 of V-st pattern—27 (29, 31) sc, and 26 (28, 30) ch-1 sps.

Row 3: With B, work Row 2 of V-st pattern, change to A in last st—54 (58, 62) dc.

Rows 6 and 7: With A, work next 2 rows of V-st pattern, change to B in last st on last row.

Rows 8 and 9: With B, work next 2 rows of V-st pattern, change to A in last st on last row.

Instructions continued on page 16.

Rep last 4 rows until piece measures 4 (4$^1/_2$, 5$^1/_2$)"/10 (11.5, 14)cm from beginning, end with a WS row (Row 3 of V-st pattern).

Shape Hood
Note: Continue to change color every other row throughout.

Row 1 (RS): Ch 3, V-st in next 9 (10, 11) ch-1 sps, dc in next 2 ch-1 sps (these 2 dc count as 1 V-st), V-st in next 4 ch-1 sps, dc in next 2 ch-1 sps (these 2 dc count as 1 V-st), V-st in last 9 (10, 11) ch-1 sps, dc in last sc, turn—50 (54, 58) dc.

Row 2: Work Row 3 of V-st pattern—25 (27, 29) sc and 24 (26, 28) ch-1 sps.

Row 3: Ch 3, V-st in next 9 (10, 11) ch-1 sps, dc in next 2 ch-1 sps, V-st in next 2 ch-1 sps, dc in next 2 ch-1 sps, V-st in next 9 (10, 11) ch-1 sps, dc in last sc—46 (50, 54) dc.

Row 4: Work Row 3 of V-st pattern—23 (25, 27) sc and 22 (24, 26) ch-1 sps.

Row 5: Ch 3, V-st in next 9 (10, 11) ch-1 sps, dc in next 4 ch-1 sps, V-st in next 9 (10, 11) ch-1 sps, dc in last sc—42 (46, 50) dc.

Row 6: Work Row 3 of V-st pattern—21 (23, 25) sc and 20 (22, 24) ch-1 sps. Fasten off.

FINISHING
On back and both fronts, measure 4 (4$^1/_2$, 5)"/10 (11.5, 12. 5)cm down from top edge and place a marker on side edges for sleeve placement. Sew shoulder seams. Sew tops of sleeves to fronts and back, between markers. Sew sleeve and side seams.

Edging: With RS of jacket facing, join A with sc in lower front corner, to work across left front edge, work 40 (42, 44) sc evenly up front edge, 50 (52, 54) sc around neck edge, and 40 (42, 44) sc down right front edge. Fasten off.

Fold hood in half, widthwise, and sew back edges together (across last row and shaping at back of hood). Sew hood around neck edges, between markers. Sew buttons along right front, opposite buttonholes.

Using yarn needle, weave in all ends.

striped hoodie schematic

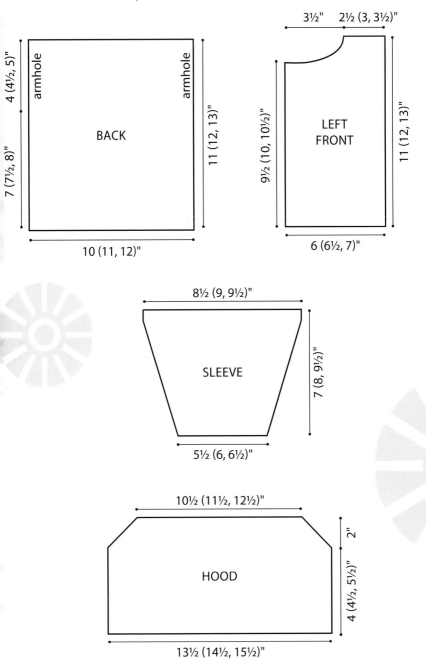

BACK
4 (4½, 5)" armhole
7 (7½, 8)"
armhole
11 (12, 13)"
10 (11, 12)"

LEFT FRONT
3½" 2½ (3, 3½)"
9½ (10, 10½)"
11 (12, 13)"
6 (6½, 7)"

SLEEVE
8½ (9, 9½)"
7 (8, 9½)"
5½ (6, 6½)"

HOOD
10½ (11½, 12½)"
2"
4 (4½, 5½)"
13½ (14½, 15½)"

17

toasty ears hat

 EASY

designed by Marilyn Losee

SIZE: 12–18 months

FINISHED MEASUREMENTS
Circumference 16"/40.5cm

MATERIALS
Caron International's Simply Soft **MEDIUM 4**
(100% acrylic; 6 oz/170g, 315 yds/288m):
Boys:
#9609 Berry Blue, 1 1/2 oz (A)
#9702 Off White, 1 oz (B)
#9755 Sunshine, 1/2 oz (C)
Girls:
#9722 Plum Wine, 1 1/4 oz (A)
#9702 Off White, 1 1/4 oz (B)
#9756 Lavender Blue, 1/2 oz (C)

Crochet hooks, one each size US G/6 (4mm) and US H/8 (5mm), or size to obtain gauge
Pom-pom maker
Embroidery needle (for Girls' Hat only)
Yarn needle

GAUGE
In single crochet, using US H/8 (5mm) hook, 8 sts and 8 rows = 2"/5cm.

ABBREVIATIONS
rep	repeat
RS	right side
rnd(s)	round(s)
sk	skip

Instructions continued on page 20.

SPECIAL TERMS

sc2tog: Single crochet 2 together—Insert hook in next stitch, yarn over and pull up a loop, (2 loops on hook), insert hook in next stitch, yarn over and pull up a loop, yarn over and draw through all 3 loops on hook.

3-dc cluster: 3 double crochet cluster—Yarn over, insert hook in next stitch, yarn over and pull up a loop (3 loops on hook), yarn over and draw through 2 loops on hook (2 loops on hook). [Yarn over, insert hook in same stitch, yarn over and pull up a loop, yarn over and draw through 2 loops on hook] twice. Yarn over and draw through all 4 loops on hook.

SPECIAL TECHNIQUE

Adjustable-ring method — Wrap yarn into a ring, ensuring that the tail falls behind the working yarn. Between finger and thumb, grip ring and tail firmly. Insert hook through center of ring, yarn over (with working yarn) and draw up a loop. Yarn over and draw through loop on hook (first chain stitch made). Work stitches of first round in the ring. After the first round of stitches is worked, pull gently, but firmly, on tail to tighten ring.

STITCHES USED

Chain (ch)
Single crochet (sc)
Slip stitch (sl st)

NOTES

1. Hat is made in one piece from the top down to the earflaps. There is no sewing required.
2. To change color, fasten off old color and join new color with slip stitch in same stitch as join of previous round.

HAT

With larger hook and A, ch 5; join with sl st in first ch to form a ring.

Rnd 1 (RS): Ch 1, work 8 sc in ring; join with sl st in first sc.

Rnd 2: Ch 1, 2 sc in each sc around; join with sl st in first sc—16 sc.

Rnd 3: Ch 1, [sc in next sc, 2 sc in next sc] 8 times; join with sl st in first sc—24 sc.

Rnd 4: Ch 1, [sc in next 2 sc, 2 sc in next sc] 8 times; join with sl st in first sc—32 sc. Change to C.

Rnd 5: Ch 1, [sc in next 3 sc, 2 sc in next sc] 8 times; join with sl st in first sc—40 sc.

Rnd 6: Ch 1, sc in each sc around; join with sl st in first sc. Change to B.

Rnd 7: Ch 1, [sc in next 4 sc, 2 sc in next sc] 8 times; join with sl st in first sc—48 sc.

Rnd 8: Ch 1, sc in each sc around; join with sl st in first sc.

Rnd 9: Ch 1, [sc in next 5 sc, 2 sc in next sc] 8 times; join with sl st in first sc—56 sc. Change to A.

Rnd 10: Ch 1, sc in each sc around; join with sl st in first sc.

Rnd 11: Ch 1, [sc in next 6 sc, 2 sc in next sc] 8 times; join with sl st in first sc—64 sc.

Rnds 12 and 13: Ch 1, sc in each sc around; join with sl st in first sc. Change to C in last sc on last row.

Rep last rnd 16 more times, working rnds in the following color sequence: 2 rnds with C, 3 rnds with B, 4 rnds with A, 2 rnds with C, 5 rnds with B. Fasten off.

EARFLAPS
Note: Work with larger hook. For Boys, work with A. For Girls, work with B.
With RS facing, sk 9 sc following join of last rnd (seam forms center back), join yarn with sl st in next sc.

Row 1: Ch 1, sc in same sc as join and next 11 sc, turn—12 sc.

Row 2: Ch 1, sc in first 5 sc, sc2tog, sc in last 5 sc, turn—11 sc.

Row 3: Ch 1, sc in each sc across, turn.

Row 4: Ch 1, sc in first 5 sc, sc2tog, sc in last 4 sc, turn—10 sc.

Row 5: Ch 1, sc in each sc across, turn.

Row 6: Ch 1, sc in first 4 sc, sc2tog, sc in last 4 sc, turn—9 sc.

Row 7: Ch 1, sc in each sc across, turn.

Row 8: Ch 1, sc in first 4 sc, sc2tog, sc in last 3 sc, turn—8 sc.

Row 9: Ch 1, sc in first 3 sc, sc2tog, sc in last 3 sc, turn—7 sc.

Row 10: Ch 1, sc in first 2 sc, [sc2tog] twice, sc in last sc, turn—5 sc.

Row 11: Ch 1, sc in first sc, [sc2tog] twice, turn—3 sc. Fasten off.

With RS facing, sk 22 sc following first earflap, join yarn with sl st in next sc. Rep Rows 1–11 for other earflap.

EDGING
With smaller hook, join A with sl st in join at center back.

Row 1: Ch 1, sc in next 9 sc, *work 10 sc evenly across side of earflap, work sc in next 3 sc across last row of earflap, work 10 sc evenly across other side of earflap*, sc in 22 sc across front of hat, rep from * to * to edge other earflap, sc in next 9 sc; join with sl st in first sc. Fasten off.

FINISHING
For Boys:
With A, make one 2"/5cm pom-pom and sew to top of hat.

Instructions continued on page 22.

For Girls:
With A, make one 2"/5cm pom-pom and sew to top of hat; and two 1¹/₂"/ 4cm pom-poms for ties.

Braid (work 2)
Cut 12 strands of A, 12"/30.5cm long. Thread 2 strands through each of the 3 sts across last row of each earflap. Braid the strands for about 1¹/₂–2"/4–5cm. Tie a small pom-pom to the end of each braid. Weave in ends securely.

Embroidery
Embroider lazy daisy and straight stitch design, as shown in diagram, on earflaps and around lower edge of hat.

Using yarn needle, weave in all ends.

Bobbles (work as many as desired)
With smaller hook and A, B, or C, make an adjustable ring, ch 3, work 3-dc cluster in ring. Fasten off. Pull gently, but firmly, on beginning tail to close ring.
Sew bobbles, randomly arranged, in B-colored sections of hat.

Braid (work 2)
Cut 6 strands each of A, B, and C, 12"/30.5cm long. Holding 3 strands of same color together, thread 3 strands through each of the 3 sts across last row of each earflap; thread A through 1 stitch, B through the next stitch, and C through the last stitch. Braid the strands for about 1¹/₂–2"/4–5cm, and tie firmly. Trim ends for tassels.

toasty ears embroidery diagram

**Embroidery Design
on each ear flap**

**Embroidery Designs
around lower B-colored section
Lazy Daisy petals (A) and
Straight Stitch (C) lines and crosses**

Smyrna Cross

Straight Stitch

Lazy Daisy

toasty toes baby booties

 EASY

designed by Marilyn Losee

SIZE: **12 months**

FINISHED MEASUREMENTS
Length   3 3/4"/9.5cm

MATERIALS

MEDIUM 4

Caron International's Simply Soft
(100% acrylic; 6 oz/170g, 315 yds/288m):
Boys:
#9609 Berry Blue, 1³/₄ oz (A)
#9702 Off White, 1³/₄ oz (B)
#9755 Sunshine, ¹/₄ oz (C)
Girls:
#9722 Plum Wine, 1³/₄ oz (A)
#9702 Off White, 1³/₄ oz (B)
#9756 Lavender Blue, ¹/₄ oz (C)

Crochet hooks, one each size US G/6 (4mm) and US H/8 (5mm), or size
to obtain gauge
Pom-pom maker
Yarn needle

GAUGE
In single crochet, using US H/8 (5mm) hook, 8 sts and 8 rows = 2"/5cm.

Instructions continued on page 26.

ABBREVIATIONS

RS   right side
rnd(s)   round(s)
sk   skip
st(s)   stitch(es)

SPECIAL TERM

sc2tog: Single crochet 2 together—
Insert hook in next stitch, yarn over
and pull up a loop, (2 loops on hook),
insert hook in next stitch, yarn over
and pull up a loop, yarn over and
draw through all 3 loops on hook.

STITCHES USED

Chain (ch)
Single crochet (sc)
Slip stitch (sl st)

NOTES

1. Each bootie is made in one piece
from top of cuff down to top of
foot. Sides of the foot are worked in
rounds from the edges of the top of
foot down to the sole.
2. To change color, fasten off old
color and join new color with slip
stitch in same stitch as join of
previous round.
3. Larger hook is used for cuff only.
Smaller hook is used for all other
parts of the bootie and tie.

BOOTIE (make 2)
Cuff

With larger hook and B, ch 26; taking
care not to twist ch, join with sl st in
first ch to form a ring.

Rnd 1: Ch 1, sc in each ch around;
join with sl st in first sc—26 sc.

Rnds 2–20: Ch 1, sc in each sc
around; join with sl st in first sc.
Change to smaller hook and A.

Leg

Next 8 Rnds: With smaller hook and
A, ch 1, sc in each sc around; join
with sl st in first sc.
Extend last loop and remove from
hook. If desired place a safety pin in
the loop. This loop will be picked up
again later to work the sides of the
foot. Do not fasten off A.

Top of Foot

Note: Work now progresses back and
forth in rows.

Row 1: Sk next 10 sc (following
extended loop), join B with sl st in
next sc, ch 1, sc in same sc and in
next 5 sc, turn; leave remaining sts
unworked—6 sc.

Next 7 Rows: Ch 1, sc in each sc across, turn.
Fasten off B.

Sides of Foot

Place dropped loop (from last rnd of leg) back on smaller hook.

Rnd 1: Ch 1, sc in next 10 sc (the 10 sc skipped at beginning of top of foot), work 7 sc evenly across side edge of top of foot, 2 sc in first st of last row of top of foot, sc in next 4 sc of last row of top of foot, 2 sc in last sc of last row of top of foot, work 7 sc evenly across other side edge of top of foot, sc in remaining 10 sc; join with sl st in first sc—42 sc.

Rnd 2: Ch 1, sc in each sc around; join with sl st in first sc.

Rnd 3: Ch 1, sc in first 20 sc, sc2tog, sc in last 20 sc; join with sl st in first sc—41 sc.

Rnd 4: Ch 1, sc in first 20 sc, sc2tog, sc in last 19 sc; join with sl st in first sc—40 sc.

Rnd 5: Ch 1, sc in first 19 sc, sc2tog, sc in last 19 sc; join with sl st in first sc—39 sc.

Rnd 6: Ch 1, sc in first 19 sc, sc2tog, sc in last 18 sc; join with sl st in first sc—38 sc.

Sole

Rnd 7: Ch 1, working in back loops only, [sc in next 3 sc, sc2tog] 7 times, sc in last 3 sc; join with sl st in first sc—31 sc.

Rnd 8: Ch 1, [sc in next 2 sc, sc2tog] 7 times, sc in last 3 sc; join with sl st in first sc—24 sc.

Rnd 9: Ch 1, [sc in next sc, sc2tog] 7 times, sc in last 3 sc; join with sl st in first sc—17 sc.
Fasten off leaving a long tail.

Sew sole seam with long end.
Weave in end securely.

FINISHING

Using yarn needle, weave in all ends. Turn top of cuff down and sl st or sew in place.

Tie (make 2)

With C, make four 1$\frac{1}{2}$"/4cm pom-poms. With B and smaller hook, ch 50. Fasten off leaving a long tail. Use the tails to sew a pom-pom to each end of each tie. Sew center of chain to top center of cuff, and tie into a bow.

.

swing jacket

■■■▢ INTERMEDIATE   *designed by Kj Hay*

SIZES: 3–6 (9-12, 18-24) months

FINISHED MEASUREMENTS
Chest 21$\frac{1}{2}$ (23$\frac{1}{2}$, 25$\frac{1}{2}$)"/54.5 (59.5, 68)cm
Length 10 (11, 12)"/25.5 (28, 30.5)cm

MATERIALS
Caron International's Simply Soft **MEDIUM 4**
(100% acrylic; 6 oz/170g, 315 yds/288m):
#9722 Plum Wine, 7 (8, 9) oz

Crochet hook, size US J-10 (6 mm), or size to obtain gauge.
Yarn needle
1 button—$\frac{5}{8}$–$\frac{3}{4}$"/16–19mm diameter
Sewing needle and matching thread

GAUGE
In pattern stitch, 14 sts and 12 rows = 4"/10cm.

ABBREVIATIONS
rep	repeat
rnd(s)	round(s)
RS	right side
sk	skip
sp(s)	space(s)
st(s)	stitch(es)

SPECIAL TERMS
sc3tog: Single crochet 3 together—[Insert hook in next stitch or space, yarn over and draw up a loop] 3 times, yarn over and draw through all 4 loops on hook.

Instructions continued on page 30.

sc5tog: Single crochet 5 together—[Insert hook in next stitch or space, yarn over and draw up a loop] 5 times, yarn over and draw through all 6 loops on hook.

STITCHES USED

Chain (ch)
Single crochet (sc)
Slip stitch (sl st)

Trinity Stitch (multiple of 2 sts + 1)
Note: The stitches of Trinity Stitch overlap. When working an sc3tog, always begin in same stitch as last leg of previous sc3tog (or same stitch as previous sc). Work last sc in same stitch as last leg of last sc3tog.

Row 1: Ch 1, sc in first st, beginning in same st as previous sc, sc3tog, ch 1, beginning in same st as last leg of previous sc3tog, sc3tog, *ch 1, beginning in same st as last leg of previous sc3tog, sc3tog; rep from * across, sc in last st (same st as last leg of last sc3tog), turn. **Note:** Do not work a ch 1 between the first sc and next sc3tog, and do not work a ch 1 between the last sc3tog and last sc. Rep Row 1 for Trinity Stitch.

NOTES

1. Jacket is worked in one piece from lower edge up to armholes. Piece is then divided, and fronts and back worked separately.
2. After shoulders are seamed, the sleeves are worked in rounds, directly into armholes.

BODY

Ch 84 (92, 98).

Row 1 (RS): Sc in 2nd ch from hook, beginning in same ch as previous sc, sc3tog, beginning in same ch as last leg of previous sc3tog, sc3tog, *ch 1, beginning in same ch as last leg of previous sc3tog, sc3tog; rep from * across, sc in last ch (same ch as last leg of last sc3tog), turn—83 (91, 97) sts.

Rows 2-7: Work in Trinity Stitch.

Note: Continue to overlap stitches throughout. Begin each sc3tog or sc5tog in same stitch as last leg of previous sc3tog (or same stitch as previous sc). Work last sc in same stitch as last leg of last sc3tog.

Row 8 (decrease row): Ch 1, sc in first st, sc3tog, [ch 1, sc3tog] 8 (9, 10) times, ch 1, sc5tog, ch 1, sc3tog, [ch 1, sc3tog] 18 (20, 21) times, ch 1, sc5tog, ch 1, sc3tog, [ch 1, sc3tog] 8 (9, 10) times, sc in last st (same as last leg of last sc3tog), turn—79 (87, 93) sts.

Rows 9–15: Work in Trinity Stitch.

Row 16 (decrease row): Ch 1, sc in first st, sc3tog, [ch 1, sc3tog] 7 (8, 9) times, ch 1, sc5tog, ch 1, sc3tog, [ch 1, sc3tog] 18 (20, 21) times, ch 1, sc5tog, ch 1, sc3tog, [ch 1, sc3tog] 7 (8, 9) times, sc in last st, turn—75 (83, 89) sts.

Work even in Trinity Stitch until piece measures 6 (6½, 7)"/15 (16.5, 18) cm. Do not fasten off.

First Front

Row 1: Ch 1, sc in first st, continue in Trinity Stitch over next 18 (20, 22) sts, working sc in same st as last leg of last sc3tog worked; leave remaining sts unworked for back and second front—19 (21, 23) sts.

Work in Trinity Stitch over these 19 (21, 23) sts only, until piece measures 9 (10, 11)"/23 (25.5, 28)cm from beginning.

Shape Neck

Row 1: Ch 1, sl st over first 9 (11, 11) sts, ch 1, sc in same st as last sl st, continue in Trinity Stitch across—11 (11, 13) sts.

Rows 2 and 3: Work in Trinity Stitch. Fasten off.

Back

Row 1: Sk next unworked st following first front, join yarn with sc in next ch-1 sp, continue in Trinity Stitch over next 34 (38, 40) sts, working sc in same st as last leg of last sc3tog worked; leave remaining sts unworked for second front—35 (39, 41) sts.

Work in Trinity Stitch over these 35 (39, 41) sts until piece measures same as first front. Fasten off.

Second Front

Row 1: Sk next unworked st following back, join yarn with sc in next ch-1 sp, continue in Trinity Stitch across—19 (21, 23) sts.

Work in Trinity Stitch over these 19 (21, 23) sts until piece measures same as first front to neck shaping.

Shape Neck

Row 1: Work in Trinity Stitch over first 11 (11, 13) sts; leave remaining sts unworked.

Rows 2 and 3: Work in Trinity Stitch. Fasten off.

Sleeve (work 2)

Sew shoulder seams.

Rnd 1: With RS facing, join yarn with sc in unworked st at underarm, working in ends of rows around armhole edge work 12 (14, 16) repeats of Trinity Stitch around, working sc in same sp as last leg of last sc3tog; join with sl st in first sc, turn—25 (29, 33) sts.

Rnd 2: Work in Trinity Stitch around; join with sl st in first sc, turn.

Rep last rnd until sleeve measures 6 (7, 8)"/15 (18, 20.5)cm. Fasten off.

FINISHING

With RS facing, join yarn with sc in lower first front corner. Work sc evenly spaced up front edge, around neck edge, and down second front edge, working a buttonloop at right front neck as follows: (sc, ch 3, sc) in corner, and working 2 sc in left front neck corner. Fasten off. Sew button to corner of neck, opposite buttonloop. Weave in all ends.

swing jacket schematic

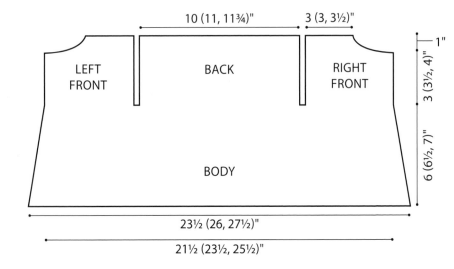

10 (11, 11¾)"   3 (3, 3½)"

LEFT FRONT   BACK   RIGHT FRONT

1"

3 (3½, 4)"

6 (6½, 7)"

BODY

23½ (26, 27½)"

21½ (23½, 25½)"

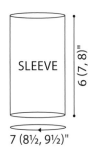

SLEEVE

6 (7, 8)"

7 (8½, 9½)"

We have made every effort to ensure that these instructions are accurate and complete. We cannot, however, be responsible for human error, typographical mistakes or variations in individual work.